21 DAYS

OF

CHARGING UP

(A Devotional for Personal Revival)

TOYIN TAIWO

Books may be purchased by contacting the Author and Publisher at:
publisher@exousiacreations.co.uk

Publishing Consultant, Cover and Interior Design:
Hadar Creations
Publisher: Exousia Creations

ISBN: 978-1-7399917-0-8

CONTENTS

FOREWORD

21 DAYS OF CHARGING UP

What do you do when you realise your spiritual batteries have run flat? It's a mistake to simply try harder, as if by our own power we can lift ourselves back to a place of spiritual vitality.

The only remedy is to 'plug in' to God, our power source, through prayer. When we're at a place of low faith energy we need help to do that, and Pastor Toyin Taiwo has produced a wonderful resource that provides just the kind of support required.

As you read and apply 21 Days of Charging Up, you will be led through a carefully designed set of prayer practices that are rooted in Scripture. You can engage at a level you can manage. If you don't know what to pray, don't worry! Pastor Toyin has detailed points for prayer and extra scripture passages to use once you feel able to go further.

Day by day, the themes for prayer open up pathways to receive God's power, charging us up and making us ready for a life of vibrant faith and effective service in God's kingdom.

Rev. Dr. Rick Lewis

Mentor, Consultant and Author of 'Mentoring Matters'

DEDICATION

I dedicate this book to my Saviour, Redeemer, Author and the Finisher of my faith. He is the Bishop of my soul, Helper and the Lifter up of my head. My Love and my Life, who loves me enough to die for me, and has graciously called and anointed me despite who I am.

Your Majesty, I can only bow – I live to serve You.

ACKNOWLEDGEMENT

I want to thank the Almighty God who saved me by His power and has sustained me till today. I thank God for making my life an epitome of grace; nothing deserved, nothing earned, nothing qualified for, yet he works daily in my life

I thank God for the people He puts in my life over the last four (4) decades of my journey in the Lord

I want to thank my mentors:
Pastor Sonny Wogu who has appeared at every important junction in my Christian walk and ministry to give support and direction and has been used by God to launch me into Pastoral ministry

Pastor Musa Bako, my father and guide in my UK ministry journey and has been used by God to bless my ministry and family in tremendous ways for the past 15 years

Pastor Funke Adeaga - my mentor in every aspect of ministry and family life. Thank you for your compassionate mentorship and prayer

Rick Lewis whom the Lord has used to discover and activate the gifts and inner treasures deposited in me; and has been a great support system to the church I was graced to oversee

Mummy Faith Okhuoya - God has used her as a pillar of intercessory support for me and my ministry.

Pastors Bioye and Biodun Segun for your inspiring leadership in the Region I was planted and for the opportunities granted to serve, grow and blossom.

Also, I want to appreciate these amazing people in my life for the covenant relationship we share:

Pastors Mathias and Hilda Akhideno for your belief in me and covenant partnership and friendship in the last 2 decades

Thank you, Vesta Thompson - my beloved friend and sister and cheer leader. I appreciate your love, friendship, and prayer support for the past 10 years

I'm also grateful to the leaders and members of Grace Chapel (RCCG) Chesterfield. I am proud to be one of you and being your Pastor has been inspiring and blissful –You are the best

Leaders and members of the Encounter Prayerline – your labour of love in these past years is highly appreciated

Shout out to my beloved sisters and co-workers in the vineyard - Ebun Adenuga, Rosemary Mohammed, and Dorothy Steve for recording, scribing, and transcribing the Charging Up sessions

A big thank you to my children and cheer leaders – we did it! Special thanks to my amiable and supportive husband, I enjoy the grace of doing life with you and I love you.

Toyin Taiwo

December 2021

INTRODUCTION

The one challenge that the body of Christ face today is lukewarmness, lethargy, worldliness, compromise, backsliding and more

There is so much lawlessness in the world and Christians are fainting and losing heart. Our only adversary throws against us all manner of temptations, attacks, seductions, afflictions to bring discouragement, disappointments, guilt, pain and suffering in order to weaken our fellowship with God

Matthew 24:12(NKJV) says, "*And because lawlessness will abound, the love of many will grow cold*". We are seeing this scripture being fulfilled in our very eyes

Evil abounds in the world and a lot of Christians are getting weary and some are struggling to sustain a consistent prayer life and intimacy with God

Many have gone into spiritual slumber and have become preys to the enemy

We need personal and individual revival!

In October 2020, the Lord drew my attention to this reawakening and instructed us to embark on a 365 day of speaking in tongues and listening to him. We ministered to the Lord daily and He built us up spiritually and dealt with other aspects of our lives as well

In the last 365 days we had experience the power of God in diverse ways. We have received more freedom in our souls, heavens has been opened, and there has been consistent divine visitation, baptism by the Holy Spirit and distribution of diverse gifts of the Spirit. Many have grown in leaps and bounds as you will read in the three (3) recorded testimonies below

Jude 1:20 **(NKJV)** says *But you, beloved, building yourselves up on your most holy faith, praying in the Holy Spirit*

As you speak in tongues and pray the word of God daily, power will be released upon you which would open channels of interaction between you and God. And as sweet fellowship with God evolves, growth will be kick started and you will be built up daily

Every battery needs charging or else it goes flat. This is the same with our spiritual lives. We need consistent charging up so that we are not deflated spiritually and only go through the motions

This book is a manual and guide which will kick-start you on a journey of revival, renewal, and recharging

Psychologists once said that, 'Whatsoever you do for up to 21 days becomes a habit'

I pray that "Charging Up" will become a perpetual habit that will take you to greater depths in your relationship with your Saviour and Redeemer

This book is a foretaste of the experience of the 365 days of "Charging up" in God's presence. I commend you to God and to the word of His grace, which is able to build you up. Amen.

14

TESTIMONIES

<u>Testimony 1</u>

*Without a doubt my life has been tremendously enriched both physically and spiritually. I joined **Charging Up** 2 months after it started*

*From the Spiritual angle, aside my first year of conversion in 1990, I cannot remember a time I have read my bible so much! The increase in hunger for the word has been tremendous. I often read the bible while praying in tongues during **Charging Up***

An amazing thing I have discovered is how God allows my mind to engage with the word while at the same time my spirit prays in tongues. During these times I write a lot and the Lord gives me messages

The Charging Up Prayer Session passes so quickly I eventually understand how it is possible to be caught up in prayer for hours. I often easily read and pray for an additional hour after it ends at 7am. Generally, I have grown in desire, content, and length of prayer over the seven months of these sessions than at any other time in my Christian life

*I have also been promoted at work since coming on **Charging Up**. The miracle of this promotion was the one I wasn't even expecting. I had told myself I wasn't going to take on further responsibilities because I didn't want any more stress at work.*

But a job came up which I half-heartedly expressed an interest in. I applied and they wrote back to me that I had not met the criteria

*Few weeks later, declarations were made on **Charging Up** on 25 July 2021. God said his children would enter a season of prosperity. They would build houses and inhabit them. Three Days prayers were made from Jeremiah 32:27 "I am the Lord, the God of all mankind, is anything too hard for me to do"*

We prayed against failure, barrenness, and lack of progress. On 9th August 2021, I received an offer for a Higher Executive Officer job, the same job I had been told I had not met the criteria! It has been a stress-free job working from home and likely to continue that way

*I believe many things have "shifted" in the spiritual realm because of praying daily on **Charging Up**. There is a longing for the altar of prayer, power for holiness and exploring new frontiers of spirituality. I feel God's presence. It is a blessing.*

M. Kay

Sheffield. UK

Testimony 2

The Charging Up experience has been a life-changing journey for me and my family. It has piqued my interest in God's manifold presence, leading in continual Koinonia with Him.

My Spirit-man has been rejuvenated, powered up, and revived as a result of my participation in this session.

Charging Up puts me in the right side of the day, like a two-edged sword, drawing God's daily benefits towards me and at the same time shielding me from the fiery dart of the enemy! Amen!

Charging up feels the same for our family's overall spiritual well-being, and it acts as a defence weaponry/ survival tactics against the ills of the day for us since it happens in the morning

Now, even when we are unable to make the meeting, there is this yearning to continually self-recharge!

This is the way to go for such times as we are, where the enemy plagues the world with depression, metal health and other psychometric disorder because it (the devil) knows that once the human mind is captured, victory is compromised! God forbid!

Indeed as a man thinks in his heart, so is he!

Charging Up *-- tested & proven.... Highly Recommended!*

Patrick S
Abu Dhabi. UAE

Testimony 3

All Glory to God for His mercies and grace upon my life

*We started **Charging Up** in November 2020 and it was like heaven opened above me in another dimension. In March, I decided to wait on the Lord for few weeks. I listed my prayer points early in the morning*

*When I got to **Charging Up,** the major and paramount one in my mind was mentioned and the exact scripture I used to pray was quoted. I didn't think much of it as it has happened many times that*

I would pray about a matter, and it is mentioned whenever I attend the session

However, what surprised me most was that I went back and added to my prayer list. The 2nd day, everything on my list plus more was mentioned in a way that I know it is me, because in the word of knowledge that came, God said what you did not ask for I have given you

I believe and I know that I will yet see more of the goodness of the Lord in the land of the living and there shall be total manifestation of all that God has promised

One morning during one of the sessions, a word of knowledge came about forgiveness, and there were members of my family I was not talking to because of pain and hurts of 10 years

Then one of my uncles that came on visit to UK called me and started talking to me about ending the 10 years animosity between my siblings and I. To the glory of God, the issues were resolved and the relationship restored

Also in April, I had a terrible accident that could have claimed my life, but I was spared because of the prayers of the Saints

I sought the face of the Lord for answers, my disobedience was revealed and God's faithfulness was proven to me. I repented and like Job, God replaced the loss with more than triple

One of the lessons I learnt is that if God had allowed me to die in the accident, I don't think I would have made eternity with Him due to unforgiveness I harboured

I thank God for giving me the opportunity to make amends and the grace to let go of all the pains. To Him be all the glory

Charging Up has changed my life tremendously. May God's name be forever praised

Olu A. (Chesterfield UK)

HOW TO USE THIS BOOK FOR PERSONAL REVIVAL

- Speak in tongues for 30 minutes

- Worship the Lord

- Listen to what God is saying to you

- Read out scripture in the manual

- Pray the prayers in the manual

- Read and pray with other scriptures as led by the Holy Spirit

- Study the Scriptural basis for prayers for each day and meditate on them

- Be Consistent

DAY 1

THANKSGIVING FOR MY SALVATION

Worship

Today's Scripture and Meditation

Psalms 100:4-5: Enter into His gates with thanksgiving, And into His courts with praise. Be thankful to Him and bless His name. For the Lord is good; His mercy is everlasting, and His truth endures to all generations

Prayers:

- My Father and my God, I enter into Your gates with thanksgiving in my heart and into Your courts with praises on my lips

- I thank and bless Your Holy Name because You are good; Your mercy is from everlasting to everlasting extending to all generations

- You are the Almighty God and there is none like you. Your glory fills the heavens! I will praise Your Name forever, for You have all wisdom and power

- You are the self-existing God, the creator of all things, our help and our shield. Our hearts rejoice in You, for we trust in Your holy name

- I thank You for You have performed many wonders for me. Your plans for me are good

- The all-knowing God; power belongs to You, to give wisdom to the wise, to give knowledge to those who have understanding

- You are the only God and You have no equal! If we tried to recite all Your wonderful deeds we would never come to an end

- Thank You for Your unfailing love in the morning and Your faithfulness in the evening

- Thank You for the privilege of a new beginning. Thank You for all You have done in my life including those I do not know about. I praise You for Your faithfulness and covenant loyalty to me. I praise You Jesus

- Thank You for keeping Your covenant with me throughout the years

- Father God, I give You thanks and praise you for Your amazing gift of salvation and for keeping me in the faith thus far

- Father, I thank You for sending Your only begotten son, Jesus Christ to this world to die for me for the forgiveness of my sins

- Thank You for enlightening my heart to say "yes" to You when You called me to be your child

- Thank You for revealing yourself to me as the way, the truth and the life, the one who has the name through which all are saved.

- You have the name above all names; at your name every knee bows and all confesses that Jesus is Lord to the glory of God the Father.

- I appreciate You for translating me from the kingdom of darkness to the kingdom of your dear son which is the kingdom of light

- I thank You for Your deliverance from the hand of the enemy that I may serve You without fear, being set apart and in right standing before You all my days

- I surrender all to You, take my life and let it be as You have ordained it from the foundation of the world.

- Thank You my Saviour, my Master and my Lord in Jesus name

Scriptures for further Prayers:

I Thessalonians 5:18, John 3:16, Psalms 107:1-2

DAY 2

THANKSGIVING FOR HIS WONDOROUS WORKS

Worship

Today's Scripture and Meditation

Psalm 107:15: *Oh! That men would give thanks to the Lord for His goodness, And for His wonderful works to the children of men!*

Psalm 118:29: *Oh, give thanks to the Lord, for He is good! For His mercy endures forever*

Prayers:

- Father, thank You for Your mercy that endures forever

- All Creation give you praise. The son, the moon, and the stars You flung in their courses

- Every creature, every plant, every rock and grain of sand proclaims the glory of its Creator, You are the

God of wonders beyond the galaxies. You alone are genuinely great.

- Thank You for the beauty of the flowers that bloom, for tender grass so fresh, for the birds that sing and hum of the bees, for the fragrant air and cooling breeze, for every new morning with its light, for health and food, for love and friends, for everything your goodness brings. For everything, Lord I say thank You

- Lord I thank You for always renewing Your mercies and love for us every morning

- Thank You for being our defence and the God of our mercy

- Father, thank You for Your sufficient grace and mercy over my life

- Father, Thank You for showing me mercy and for giving me grace to help me in my times of need

- Thank You for Your blessings and gift of grace that cover all of my faults. I will give thanks and praise to the Lord, for He is a great God and the rock of my salvation

- I praise and bless You for all Your goodness and mercies over my life and family

- Father, I thank You for You have never left me nor forsaken me, You fight my battles and have not given me as prey to the teeth of the enemy

- Thank You for not allowing the rod of the wicked to fall on me. You restrained me for being a victim of the works of darkness

- Thank You Lord for being my refuge from the storm and shelter from the heat, my shield, my fortress, my strong tower and my hiding place

- Thank You for frustrating all the plans of our adversaries, shielding me and giving me victories and increase on every side

- Thank You for all the journey mercies and sustaining mercy that You have always granted us

- Thank You for all the spiritual and physical enrichment in my life

- Thank You for all Your wondrous works in my life. You are the Lord of heaven and earth

Scriptures for further Prayers:

Lamentation. 3:22, Ps. 59:17, Psalm 124:2-3 & 6, 1 Chronicles 16:8-9

DAY 3

THANKSGIVING FOR DAILY BENEFIT

Worship

Today's Scripture and Meditation

Psalm 103:1-2: Bless the Lord, O my soul; And all that is within me, bless His holy name! Bless the Lord, O my soul, and forget not all His benefits:

Prayers:

- Almighty God, I thank You for Your goodness, faithfulness and truth in our lives that endures through all generations

- Thank You for Your strength and empowerment through the years

- Father, I thank You for granting my request and meeting my demands

- Thank You, Lord, for all the spiritual resources given to me; filling me with Your Holy Spirit for the assignment, protecting me under Your blood, and for giving us Your name as a backing authority

- Thank You for all Your benefits bestowed on me

- I thank you for the benefit of Your covenant and all the covenant blessings; for healing my diseases and for health, for the provision of all my needs, for victories in all battles

- Thank you for Your grace and mercy, for life, for safety and security

- Thank You for Your peace that surpasses all understanding

- Thank You for all Your benefits that You load us with daily

- Father, I thank You for all the signs, wonders and miracles that You have worked in my life. You are the Lord of heaven and earth. You are the God of wonders beyond the galaxies.

- Thank You for Your powerful name, thank You for healing in my body when I needed it, Thank You for destroying the power of the enemy and preventing any deadly thing to harm me. I thank You for all Your miracles in my life. I will proclaim Your wonders tirelessly, for You alone deserve the glory and honour

- Father, I thank You because You are the God of possibilities

- I thank you for Your compassion, goodness, faithfulness and truth that endures throughout all generations in Jesus name.

- I thank you and praise You my Lord, for You are a great God

- Thank You Father, for the blood of Jesus that is available to wash us whiter than snow, from all our sins.

- Thank You for the blood of Jesus that speaks better things over my life

- Thank You Father for the blood of Jesus that purges our conscience from dead works to serve the living God

- Thank You Father for Your goodness and mercy that follow me always

Scriptures for further Prayers:

Psalm. 136:1, Revelations 7:14, Hebrews 12:24, Hebrews 9:14-15, Psalm 23:6

DAY 4

MERCY AND FORGIVENESS

Worship

Today's Scripture and Meditation

I John 1:8-I0: If we say that we have no sin, we deceive ourselves, and the truth is not in us. If we confess our sins, He is faithful and just to forgive us our sins and to cleanse us from all unrighteousness. If we say that we have not sinned, we make Him a liar, and His word is not in us

Prayers:

- Father I thank You because You are full of mercy

- Thank You for the blood of Jesus that is available to wash us whiter than snow, from all our sins

- Thank You for Your kindness in not shutting the door of mercy against me

- I confess all my sins before You *(confess Your sins and repent of them)*

- Father, have mercy upon me in any way I have failed to show compassion on the wounded around me in Jesus name

- Father, have mercy upon me for my prayerlessness, lack of personal fellowship and devotion

- Father, have mercy upon me for every sin committed with my tongue. You said in your word that a man that does not offend in word is a perfect man. Since I cannot both bless and curse from the same mouth, I choose to bless always in Jesus name

- Father, have mercy upon me for dwelling in criticism, murmuring, grumbling, unbelief, double-mindedness and doubting Your word

- Father, have mercy upon me for acts of unfaithfulness in the giving of my offerings, tithe, first fruits and vows, in the payment of taxes, and other lawful national obligations

- Father, have mercy upon me for acts of disobedience to your word, my leaders, those in authority over me, traffic regulations on the highways and other governmental rules and regulations.

- Father, have mercy upon me for acts of dishonesty in keeping to my words and lack of personal integrity

- Father, have mercy on me for the sins of hatred, jealousy, unforgiveness, vengeful acts, backbiting, backstabbing, discrimination in the Church, workplace and communities

- Father, have mercy upon me for carelessness, lackadaisical attitude, laziness, nonchalant attitude to your word, the brethren and your righteous causes

- Father, have mercy upon me for the sins of ingratitude; lack of appreciation for the free gifts of nature, and for not sharing testimonies.

- Father, give me a heart to obey You in all things and to keep short accounts with you

- O Lord, I thirst for you. Quench my longing soul and refresh me by your Holy Spirit

- Your mercy is the rain on the desert of my soul, look upon me with mercy as you normally do to those who love your name

- Thank you for cleansing me from all unrighteousness according to your word

Scriptures for further Prayers:

Romans 9:15, Titus 3:2, Roman 14:23, Ezekiel 36:26

DAY 5

NO CONDEMNATION

Worship

Today's Scripture and Meditation

***Romans 8:1**: There is therefore now no condemnation to those who are in Christ Jesus, who do not walk according to the flesh, but according to the Spirit*

Prayers:

- Lord, I thank you that you took my place to go to Calvary

- I thank you that you paid all that we owed in full, on the cross when you said it is finished

- I thank you that what the law was powerless to do because of the weakness of our flesh, God did by sending his own Son, to be a sin offering for us

- Help me to rest in the truth that there is no condemnation for me because I am in you

- I thank you for adopting me as a member of your family. I am accepted and not rejected, I am justified and not condemned. I am redeemed and not in bondage

- Heavenly Father, thank You, that I am Your child, accepted in Christ and called to be fruitful. I ask that today I will live every moment of my life as unto You, bringing forth spiritual fruit that is pleasing in Your sight.

- By the law of the Spirit of life, I ask to be set me free from the law of sin and death. I pray that the Spirit of God will live in me and that I will be controlled by Him

- Help me to live according to the Spirit more, rather than the flesh so that I can yield more to the instructions and directions of the Holy Spirit

- Though my body are dead because of sin, may my spirit be alive because of your righteousness

- In You I have redemption, that is, I have deliverance and salvation through Your blood, which paid the penalty for my sins and resulted in the forgiveness and my complete pardon, which is according to the riches of Your grace that You lavished on me

- My old self [my human nature] was nailed to the cross with Christ, in order that my body of sin might be done away with, so that I am no longer a slaves to sin.

- I cast out every guilt and rejection. I recognise God as my father and cry "Abba, Father," I rejoice in my status as heir of God and co-heir with Christ

- I thank you that you will not condemn those who are in Christ Jesus. I am not condemned, I will not be condemned, and I cannot be condemned

- I pray that the Spirit of God that raised Jesus from the dead will live in me and that God will give life to our mortal bodies through that same Spirit of Life

- I surrender to be led by the Spirit, to put to death the misdeeds of the body through the Spirit and find life as a child of God

Scriptures for further Prayers

Romans 6:1-7, Romans 8:11, Ephesians 1:7-8

DAY 6

SEEKING GOD

Worship

Today's Scripture and Meditation

Jeremiah 29:13: And You will seek me and find me, when You search for Me with all Your heart

Prayers:

- Father, I come seeking You today. You are my Lord, You are my Saviour. I love You my God with all my heart, with all my soul, and with all my mind

- I worship and adore You. I am awestruck by who You are. You are light and life, grace and mercy, just and right, and filled with love and power

- I seek your face, let my heart draw near to You. You said we should seek You first and this is all I want to do Lord. I seek You with all my heart because I know that my desires are found in You and will be fulfilled in You

- As the deer pants for the water brooks so I pant after You Lord. I thirst for You and want to be filled by You

- I surrender all to you and give everything to you just to know You more, Lord. You desire a relationship and so I say; Yes Lord

- Reveal Yourself to me afresh. As I seek Your face, let me find You.

- I need to know You personally, face-to-face as Moses did: the real You, not some image I already picture in my mind.

- I want to do more than lip service to you, I want to know, love and obey you

- I chose to draw close to you Lord and ask that you draw close to me

- Help me to know Your voice and to respond when You call, Lord

- I call to you, Lord, answer and tell me of great and hidden things that I have not known. You long to fill me with the knowledge and desire for your will. Speak to me, let me know your heart and how you feel

- Holy Spirit, reveal the perfect plans of our heavenly Father to me in Jesus name

Scriptures for further prayers

2 Chronicles 7:14, Matthew 22:37, Matthew 6:33

DAY 7

HOLY SPIRIT ENDUEMENT

Worship

Today's Scripture and Meditation

Acts 2:1-4: When the Day of Pentecost had fully come, they were all with one accord in one place. And suddenly there came a sound from heaven, as of a rushing mighty wind, and it filled the whole house where they were sitting…And there appeared unto them cloven tongues like as of fire, and it sat upon each of them. And they were all filled with the Holy Ghost, and began to speak with other tongues, as the Spirit gave them utterance

Prayers:

- Father God, I come to you today in the name of your Son Jesus, asking that you baptise and fill me afresh with the Holy Ghost as it was on the day of Pentecost

- Lord, release your presence over my life afresh and ignite your fire in me

- Holy Spirit come upon me break my walls down, infiltrate, penetrate, invade and rule my life

- Let the power of the Highest overshadow me so that Christ may be fully formed in me
- Father, incubate me with fire of the Holy Spirit, in Jesus' name.
- Let there be the manifestation of the Spirit transforming power in my life
- Fill me up with fresh fire, fresh grace, fresh anointing that I may impact the world around me for you
- Let the Spirit of God quicken my mortal body in a supernatural manner
- As you transformed the timid and fearful disciples, Lord transform me to be a bold, fearless witness for you
- Ignite your fire within me, Oh Lord
- Let there be a spiritual disruption by the power of the Spirit in my life and through me
- Father, let me not receive your spirit and power and be mute. Let there be unusual manifestations that will cause the non-Christian community to pay attention to You in me
- Enable me under the unction of your spirit, let me grab the attention of everyone in my proximity for Christ
- Transform me into spaces that ignite conviction about the gospel in order to change people's lives and direction.
- Let me be continually filled with Joy and the Holy Spirit in Jesus name

Scriptures for further prayers

1 Corinthians 4:7a, Luke 1:35, Joel 2:28, Acts 13:52

DAY 8

AN OVERFLOW

Worship

Today's Scripture and Meditation

John 7: 37-39: On the last day, that great day of the feast, Jesus stood and cried out, saying, "If anyone thirsts, let him come to Me and drink. He who believes in Me, as the Scripture has said, out of his heart will flow rivers of living water. But this He spoke concerning the Spirit, whom those believing in Him would receive; for the Holy Spirit was not yet given, because Jesus was not yet glorified

Prayer:

- Father Lord I believe in you, I believe you came and died. You were buried and resurrected for my sake

- Lord I thirst for you, I long to be filled by Your spirit and to be in Your presence. My soul waits on You, Father, draw me close to you

- Brood over my life and let every area that manifest darkness receive light. Let there be more light in my soul

- Let there be order and orderliness, where there has been voidness, replace it with the fullness of you till the emptiness disappears

- Fill me afresh Lord and fill me till there is an overflowing

- Let there be a living and continual fountain of the Holy Spirit in my life

- Lord open and display the hidden treasures of God in me

- Let there be an abundance of Your Spirit and an overflow of the abundance of You in my life

- Let the living water flow over my soul, Let the Holy Spirit take perfect control

- Let the fountain that never grows dry, nor ceases, flow continually into me, around me and through me

- Let there be an abundant outpouring of your spirit in my life, to the extent that out of my belly shall flow rivers of living water

- Take me to a new level of intimacy with you, where I will live in the overflow of your Spirit

- Pour out your spirit upon me Lord; Let fresh grace, fresh unction, fresh anointing be released. Fill me afresh Lord

- I will seek you God to fill me with all joy and peace as I trust in You that I may flow unto others by the power of the Holy Spirit at work in me.

- I want more of you; I am desperate for you because without you I am nothing and I am lost; Jesus! More of you Lord!

- Overshadow me Lord. Not my will but yours in Jesus name

Scriptures for further prayers
Isaiah 44:3-4; Joel 3:18. Genesis 1:1-3

DAY 9

WARFARE

Worship

Today's Scripture and Meditation

Colossians 2:14 (AMP): Having cancelled out the certificate of debt consisting of legal demands [which were in force] against us and which were hostile to us. And this certificate He has set aside and completely removed by nailing it to the cross

Prayers:

- Thank you, Lord, for the finished work on the cross for my sake; taking curses out of the way and nailing every record of charges that was against me to the cross

- I challenge every certificate of debt consisting of legal demands which were in forces against me and which were hostile to me, with the blood of Jesus. According to the word of God, this certificate has been set aside and completely removed by nailing it to the cross

- Every legal ground of the enemy in my life is broken and all accusations are destroyed in Jesus name

- Father disarm every ruler and authority - those supernatural forces of evil operating against us - working against my faith in God. Make a public example of them, triumph over them in my life by the reason of the cross.

- I command all heads of gates and everlasting doors, preventing the presence and manifestation of God, the King of glory, in my life to be lifted. Let the King of glory come into my life

- I bind every strong man and dispossess them of any grounds or territories taken. I command the release, restoration and resurrection of all that the enemy has stolen, killed or destroyed

- Every stronghold of the enemy preventing a consistent Christian walk, prayer life and ministry, is destroyed in Jesus name

- Let every clog in my spiritual wheel be flushed out by the blood of Jesus

- I frustrate the token of the liars and the deceiver of the brethren

- I bind every monitoring spirit and destroy every monitoring apparatus with which my life is been monitored in the spirit in Jesus name

- I connect with the covenant that I have with God in the blood of Jesus and claim the covenant blessings in Jesus name

- Blessed be Your name oh God, in Jesus mighty name I pray. Amen.

Scriptures for further Prayers

Psalms 24:7-10, Isaiah 44:25, John 10:10

DAY 10

DELIVERANCE AND RESTORATION

Worship

Today's Scripture and Meditation

Isaiah 59:1: Behold, the Lord's hand is not shortened at all, that it cannot save, nor His ear dull with deafness, that it cannot hear.

Isaiah 49:24-25: Shall the prey be taken from the mighty, or the captives of the righteous be delivered? But thus says the Lord: "Even the captives of the mighty shall be taken away, And the prey of the terrible be delivered; For I will contend with him who contends with you, And I will save your children

Prayers:

- Lord we thank you because you are Almighty, Powerful and Awesome God

- I thank you because you are my Saviour and the Redeemer of my soul

- You are the Great Defender and Deliverer; I acknowledge that your everlasting arms are underneath me

- I bring myself and all that pertains to me under the covering of the blood of Jesus as I take the battle to the gate of the enemy with my ascertained victory, in Jesus name

- I pray to you that every area of my life will receive the light of God's deliverance, and salvation of the Lord

- Your hand is not too short to deliver, Father deliver me from every oppression and suppression of the enemy. I cry out to the Lord to deliver me

- When light shines in darkness, darkness cannot comprehend it; let the light of God shine in every facet of my life and chase darkness away in Jesus name

- I pray that everything that preys upon me or has kept me captive will loose its hold upon my life today in Jesus name

- Let every chains, limitations, snares and cords of bondage in my life (physical and spiritual) be broken in Jesus name

- Let all prison doors be opened that I might escape every oppression and suppression of the enemy in Jesus name

- Lord you were manifested to destroy the works of the enemy. I pray that every works of darkness in my life be destroyed

- By the word of the Lord I decree, "It is enough to the angel of death, it is enough to the angel of sickness, it is enough to angel of mishap, it is enough, it is enough; today is the expiry date". Today is the end of trouble, it is enough, I receive peace of God in Jesus name

- I command every stranger in my life to come out of their closed places

- I declare it is enough! That trouble is enough, that problem is enough, that sickness is enough, that failure is enough. You act no further in the name of Jesus

- Let every spirit not consistent with the Spirit of God, loose your hold upon my life. Every spirit of fear, spirit of doubt, spirit of worry, spirit of anxiety, spirit of unforgiveness, spirit of bitterness, spirit of anger, spirit of failure and stagnancy, spirit of infirmity, all demonic spirits - loose your hold in Jesus name

- Father restore all that the enemy has stolen, killed or destroyed in my life in Jesus name

- I declare the recovery and the redeem of all wasted time today in Jesus name

- Thank you Lord for You are my help, my hope and my deliverer.

- I appreciate You, Lord, in Jesus name. Amen.

Scriptures for further prayers

Galatians 5:1, Deuteronomy 33:27, Isaiah 59:1

DAY 11

SPIRITUAL VIOLENCE

Worship

Today's Scripture and Meditation

Matthew 11:12: And from the days of John the Baptist until now the kingdom of heaven suffers violence, and the violent take it by force

Prayers:

- Lord, I thank you for the grace given to me to be your child and to be called a soldier of Christ

- I come before You to draw strength, grace, capacity and to be enlarged and sharpened in the Spirit so that I will become robust in the spirit

- I understand that this race is not for the swift and it is by Your mercy. Neither can I take the enemy by my strength, so I receive daily strength to take the kingdom of God by force

- I receive the spirit of holy "violence", to fight the good fight of faith, overcome the oppression and suppression of the enemy

- I break free from the oppression and bondage of the enemy

- I take hold of eternal victory, I take hold of my deliverance, I take hold of my freedom, I take hold of all my possessions that the enemy has stolen, killed or destroyed.

- I reject being lukewarm but I receive grace and courage to forcefully take hold of the kingdom of God, to grow and to advance in it

- I take hold of the kingdom of God and I magnificently push back the frontiers of darkness.

- Let my heart be inflamed with a desire after the knowledge and obtaining of heaven and heavenly things

- Let your power in me work to produce a response so that I will not be deceived by lazy wishes and cold endeavours but be a candidate for heaven

- Let the power of the Holy Spirit quicken and enlighten me. Let my ears be opened and my heart be softened to accommodate the indwelling of the Holy Spirit

- Let every numbness in my heart and mind be uprooted by force
- Let the zeal of the Lord consume me and compel me to run with your righteous cause
- Enable me to always be on my knees in the intercessory prayer intensified by the power to take territories by force from the hold of darkness
- I receive grace not to fall away in times of tribulation and trouble but to remain steadfast, immovable, always abounding in the works of the Lord Jesus Christ
- I continue to hold on to You and continually look forward to the day of Your appearing and our reward in the name of Jesus

Scriptures for further Prayers
1 Timothy 6:12, Luke 3:15-16, I Corinthians 15:58

DAY 12

DEPENDENCY

Worship

Today's Scripture and Meditation

Proverbs 3:5-8: Trust in the Lord with all Your heart, And lean not on Your own understanding; In all Your ways acknowledge Him, And He shall direct Your paths. Do not be wise in Your own eyes; Fear the Lord and depart from evil. It will be health to Your flesh, And strength to Your bones

Prayers:

- Father Lord, I am grateful that You are my God and that You are the sovereign God. You know all things and can do all things

- Lord I come with open heart before You and I surrender all to You and Your ways; I submit to Your will and counsel and will not do evil

- Let my heart be continuously before You and always tender before You

- Give me a heart of flesh, oh God; a heart that You can reach, a heart that you can change and mould into your perfect will

- I will no longer want to depend on my own wisdom and intelligence which are limited

- I will not depend on my emotions which are unstable and cannot be trusted. I will not depend on human traditions which are selfish, self-serving and self-centred

- Lord I acknowledge the fact that without You, I can do nothing. I put all my ways before You as I acknowledge that You are the only wise God

- I pray that You direct my path and direct my steps in family, career, ministry; in the city and everywhere I go

- Give me direction that I may not miss my way, that I will not be diverted, derailed or distracted in the journey of life. I put all my trust in You, O God of my salvation.

- Uphold me with your righteous hand that I will not be deceived by the enemy to do evil

- You never make mistakes, You are never late and You do not sleep nor slumber, Lord I submit to your wise counsel at every junction, I depend on you for everything that pertain to life and godliness

- Give me the strength to depend on you at all times

- I put my hands in Yours, Lord, take me safely to shore in Jesus name

- I choose to do it your way now. I acknowledge my total dependence on you at this moment. All that I have is Yours and they all belongs to You

- All my rights of ownership are Yours because You have purchased me with a great price. Guide me into your plan and purpose

- You are all I need and You are the one I desire. I am under Your leadership. I chose to live by faith, sustain me Lord

- I depend on you for my life, Christian walk, family, calling, ministry, business, and career

- Thank You, that Christ is the source and supply of my life; I acknowledge my total dependency on you. I desire to live in total reliance on You, in thoughts, words and deeds, so that everyday of my life will be fruitful and indeed blessed

- Thank You Lord because You know how to manage my life perfectly. I give it over to you that I may continually be blessed because of You.

- Thank you Father, In Jesus name. Amen.

Scriptures for further Prayers

John 15:5b, 2 Peter 1:3, 1 Corinthians 6:20

DAY 13

HEALING FOR THE MIND

Worship

Today's Scripture and Meditation

2 Corinthians 10:4-5: For the weapons of our warfare are not carnal but mighty in God for pulling down strongholds, casting down arguments and every high thing that exalts itself against the knowledge of God, bringing every thought into captivity to the obedience of Christ

Prayers:

- Father God I thank you because you are my God in whom I trust. You are my help, my refuge, strong tower and my hiding place

- You have the name that is above every other name and according to your word, at your name every knee shall bow and every tongue shall confess that Jesus Christ is Lord to the glory of God the Father

- Lord I bow my knee to your lordship and majesty and command every knee that stands against your will and counsel in my life to bow in the name of Jesus

- I command everything that does not bring glory to your name in my life to bow in the name of Jesus

- Let every stronghold in my life be pulled down in the name of Jesus. Every stronghold of pride, fear, control, criticism, independence, resistance, sexual perversion, unbelief, quenching the Spirit, anger, competition, contention, cruelty, division, envious of others, hate, jealousy, murder, rage, fighting, quarrelling, restlessness, revenge, selfishness, spite, suspicion, wrath, conceited, provocation, controlled by own desires, strife, divisions, bitterness, envy, lying, selfish ambition, covetousness, carnality...... *(please mention the ones that apply to you)*

- Free me from the mind-set of the flesh, which is hostile to you and does not and cannot submit to you

- I refute and cast down every argument, theory, reasoning, philosophy, ideology, tradition and culture, every proud and lofty thing that sets itself up against the true knowledge of God in my life in Jesus name

- I bring into captivity every one of my thoughts to the obedience of Christ. Let every unhelpful, unwholesome, unholy and wandering thoughts *(add yours)* be taken captive to the obedience of Christ in Jesus name

- I have not received the spirit of fear but of love, of power and of sound mind. I pray for sound mind and complete healing for my mind in Jesus name

- Father let there be total freedom in my mind from every torment of the devil

- I pray for healing for every weariness, hurt, pain, stress, heart break, disappointment, rejection, anxiety, depression, panic attack, confusion, lack of concentration, memory loss, negativity, overthinking, torment, *(please mention and/or add the ones that apply to you)*

- Grant me peace of mind and calm me when my heart is troubled, give me the mind of Christ

- Father build me up when I am broken hearted; I receive the garment of praise for the spirit of heaviness, I receive joy in place of sadness, I receive peace in place of torment

- Give me the strength and clarity of mind to find my purpose and walk the path you've laid out for me

- Thank you Father for answering my prayers in Jesus name

Scriptures for further prayers

2 Timothy 1:7, Isaiah 61:1-3, Isaiah 53:5b

DAY 14

DEALING WITH THE FLESH

Worship

Today's Scripture and Meditation

Romans 6:19: I speak in human terms because of the weakness of Your flesh. For just as You presented Your members as slaves of uncleanness, and of lawlessness leading to more lawlessness, so now present Your members as slaves of righteousness for holiness.

Prayers:

- Father Lord, I thank You for saving my soul. Thank You for the daily work of the Holy Spirit to transform me

- I pray that you enable me not to live according to the flesh so that my mind will not be set on the things of the flesh but only on the things of the Spirit

- Heavenly Father, let me not be estranged from you who created me and saved me by dying on the cross to pay the price for my sins

- Lord, help me when I am covered with any worldly and fleshly shroud that may cause me to wander from

You and redirect me when I wander and pull away from you

- Deliver me from worldly thoughts, mindsets, actions, reactions, behaviour and lifestyle

- Search me Lord, and examine my heart and my attitudes. I receive strength to nail to the cross of Christ and learn to walk in spirit and truth more and more

- Draw me back and close to You anytime my fleshly desires causes me to leave my first love, the Lord Jesus Christ

- Deliver me from this fleshly mind-set that has swamped the heart of Christ. I continuously gain love and joy in your presence in Jesus name

- I am not of the world and so I cannot have confidence in the flesh but in the spirit of God

- Thank you for setting me free from slavery to sins and adopting me to be a son of God. I will bear fruits in holiness and righteousness

- I yield my members to You in obedience to You and Your word. I am in tune to the whisperings and promptings of the Holy Spirit to lead me to righteousness

- I submit my body, spirit and soul unto You. Let the flesh be silenced and not gratified in my life but let the Spirit take authority of my life

- I submit my will, plans, agenda, dreams, aspirations and ambitions; let them be overtaken by your will, plan and purpose in Jesus name

- Let my mind be set on the things of God and not the things of the flesh. Let me not be carnally minded but rather be spiritually minded so that I can have abundant life and peace.

- Lord transform my heart, ideas and perspectives; let my heart be malleable, changeable, transformable and instructable by your Spirit.

- Enable me to sow to the Spirit and not to the flesh so I do not reap corruption and destruction

- Let me not be taken over by temptation, enable me to always see and take the way of escape that you have provided for me in Jesus name

- Enable me to walk in and live by the Spirit. I am not camouflaged or disoriented by the opinions of men or the suggestions of my flesh. Holy Spirit have your way in my life; I want to be always led by you. Thank you Lord, in Jesus name. Amen

Scriptures for further prayers

Romans 8:5, Romans 6:22, Galatians 6:8

DAY 15

HEALING FOR THE BODY

Worship

Today's Scripture and Meditation

Rom 8:11: But if the Spirit of him that raised up Jesus from the dead dwell in you, he that raised up Christ from the dead shall also quicken your mortal bodies by his Spirit that dwells in you

Prayers:

- Father I thank you that you sent your Son Jesus to die for me on the cross of Calvary. Your word says that the chastisement for our peace was upon Him, and by His stripes we were healed. I stand on your word today, to claim my healing in Jesus name.

- In the scriptures, we see that the people all looked to You and power came out of You to heal them all. As I look to you this today for all manner of healing, Lord let your power flow into my body, soul and spirit to heal me

- Lord, you sent your word and healed them and delivered them from their destructions, let Your word bring healing, health and deliverance to my body in order to rescue me from destruction

- According to your word, "Heal me, Lord, and I will be healed; save me and I will be saved, for you are the one I praise."

- Bless my water and my bread, let nothing I eat or drink bring sickness or diseases to my body but let them bring healing and health to my body in Jesus name

- According to your word, Father take away every sickness away from me and my family in Jesus name

- Jesus said, "Every plant not planted by my heavenly Father will be uprooted". So I declare every planting, deposit, sickness, illness, weakness etc. in my body be uprooted, only the plantings of the lord will germinate and grow in my life in Jesus name

- Let the Sun of righteousness rise with healing wings to bring healing into my life

- Let the Spirit of God, who raised Jesus from the dead, dwell in me to quicken and give life to my mortal body. I will live and not die; I will be in glorious in Jesus name

- Father restore health to me, and heal me of any wounds (body and mind) that all can go well with me

- Thank you for answering my prayers in Jesus name. Amen.

Scriptures for further prayers

Luke 6:19, Psalms 107:20, Jeremiah 17:14, Exodus 23:25

DAY 16

FRUIT OF THE SPIRIT

Worship

Today's Scripture and Meditation

Galatians 5:22-23: But the fruit of the Spirit is love, joy, peace, longsuffering, kindness, goodness, faithfulness, gentleness, self-control. Against such there is no law

Prayers:

- Father Lord, I thank you for the grace to witness a new day, let your name be exalted in the name of Jesus

- Lord Jesus, I thank you that You have redeemed me to be conformed to the image of Christ. Lord manifest in me with the fruit of the spirit in a greater dimension that I might be like you

- Lord, break me down and remould me to the shape and size that you want, take over my entire being

- Your word says love is the greatest. Father Lord, I pray that you will teach me how to love unconditionally

- Lord, I pray that you will baptize me with your Holy Spirit and power afresh with the Spirit of love that quickens to live as God wills in the name of Jesus.

- Let love be in the foundation of all I do, let love reign in my heart and give me the grace to overlook the wrongdoings of others, to shun every negative things that people do to me in the name of Jesus.

- Father Lord, I pray that you will help me to love people genuinely, regardless of their religious beliefs, doctrine, tribe or language. Help me to look beyond traditions, cultures and all the things that separate us

- Lord, I pray for the grace to be kind to other people, Give me the grace to treat people with kindness and humility

- Father, give me the grace to control myself, that I will not be driven around by temptations of the devil but will be self-controlled

- Lord, restore unto me the joy of Your salvation and uphold me with your free spirit. I pray that you will fill my heart with the joy of the Holy Ghost no matter what I go through

- Father Lord, I pray for the grace to remain faithful to you alone and in all my dealings. The grace to fear you and obey all your instructions, directions and guidance

- Father Lord, from now, I have been redeemed to look like you

- I come against every spirit of hatred, bitterness, strife, jealousy, envy and haughtiness, and naughtiness. I rebuke every spirit of resentment and anger, bias and nepotism, segregation and discrimination and every atom of self-exaltation in me in the name of Jesus.

- Father Lord, I come against every demonic powers that is hindering me from exhibiting my full potentials as a child of God, limiting me from attaining a new level in the realm of the spirit and preventing me from bearing the fruit of the Spirit as I should, in Jesus name

- I pray that you will heighten my spiritual maturity to grow beyond every limiting factor in the name of Jesus

- I pray that you will fill my heart with love, joy and peace, longsuffering, kindness, goodness, faithfulness, gentleness, self-control. The grace to be at peace with all men, I pray that you give this to me in the name of Jesus

Scriptures for further prayers

Romans 8:29, 1 Corinthians 13:4-8a

DAY 17

THE WORD OF GOD

Worship

Today's Scripture and Meditation

Proverbs 4: 20-22: My son, give attention to my words; Incline Your ear to my sayings. Do not let them depart from Your eyes; Keep them in the midst of Your heart; For they are life to those who find them, and health to all their flesh

Prayers:

- Father Lord, thank You for not leaving us without instruction and guidance

- Thank You for Your word is a lamp unto my feet and a light unto my path

- Enable me to hear, read, study, memorize, mediate on, speak and apply your word that I might live a victorious life

- Father let your word give life to everything that are spiritually dead, change me through your word; let your word actively work in my life for conviction and change my heart and mind

- Let your word dig deep into the depths of my soul and spirit, to convict me towards life-altering changes

- Let the word of God have an incisive and penetrating quality in my life so that it lays bare self-delusions and moral false arguments

- I refute sophisticated arguments, theories and reasoning. I cast down every proud and lofty thing that sets itself up against the true knowledge of God

- By your word, strengthen my faith

- By your word, cleanse and sanctify me

- By your word, build me up

- By your word, equip me for kingdom service

- By your word, make me a fruitful believer

- By your word, strengthen me

- By your word, give me wisdom

- I pray that your word will light up my life and my path

- Your word is like fire, let your word purify and sanctify me

- Your word is like a hammer to break every fallow ground of my heart and mind

- Help me to desire the sincere milk of the word so that I can grow daily unto maturity
- I want to look into the perfect law of liberty daily to behold your glory as in a mirror and be transformed by it from glory to glory
- Let there be a performance of your every word in my life in Jesus name
- I receive grace to delight in Your word, my ears shall be open unto Your sayings in order that Your word will always be in my view, that Your word shall be in my heart always
- Your word is life to me. Let Your word be health to my body in Jesus name
- Give me an unquenchable desire for your word

Scriptures for further prayers

Deuteronomy 33:3, Ephesians 5:225-26, Joshua 1:8. Romans 12:2

DAY 18

GIFTS OF THE SPIRIT

Worship

Today's Scripture and Meditation

1 Corinthians 12:7-11: But the manifestation of the Spirit is given to each one for the profit of all: for to one is given the word of wisdom through the Spirit, to another the word of knowledge through the same Spirit, to another faith by the same Spirit, to another gifts of healings by the same Spirit, to another the working of miracles, to another prophecy, to another discerning of spirits, to another different kinds of tongues, to another the interpretation of tongues. But one and the same Spirit works all these things, distributing to each one individually as He wills

Prayers:

- Dear Lord, I thank You for sending the Lord Jesus to live and die for me, I understand that my body is the temple of the Holy Spirit, and that You have sent Him to indwell my heart to lead and guide me into all truth

- Lord, I come asking that You will manifest your gift in me for the benefit of the body of Christ

- You said to covet the best gifts; therefore I covet the gift of …. *(mention gifts from the above or other scripture as desired)*

- Let The Spirit of the LORD rest upon me, the Spirit of the fear of the Lord. I desire a reverent fear towards You. I declare that my life will be informed by your Spirit

- Let the Spirit of wisdom and understanding, the Spirit of counsel and might, the Spirit of knowledge and of the fear of the LORD manifest fully in my life

- Father Lord, let your Spirit rest on me to bring about new life, restoration, wisdom that would bring about capacity of judging rightly in matters relating to life and conduct

- Let the Spirit of the Lord rest on me bringing application of all knowledge and understanding; I declare that I know how to live my life according to the will of God

- Let the Spirit of the Lord rest on me to give me the road map of life and enable me to activate what God has already given me

- Let the Spirit of the Lord rest on me to bring divine wisdom; the kind that brings peace, the type that enables insightful choices for destiny fulfilment; the kind that would empower me to be efficient and be the leader in all areas

- Let the spirit of the Lord rest on me to bring might – the force, domination, mastery, potency and efficiency – unto me

- Let the spirit of the Lord rest on me, enabling me to run and not be weary; to walk and not faint in the might of the Lord and works of the kingdom of God

- Father grant unto me the gift of the spirit required to fulfil my purpose that I might be relevant to edify the body of Christ and depopulate the kingdom of darkness in Jesus name

Scriptures for further prayers:

Isaiah 11:2, James 3:17, 1 Corinthians 12:31

DAY 19

FRUITFULNESS

Worship

Today's Scripture and Meditation

John 15:1-5(AMPC): *I am the True Vine, and My Father is the Vinedresser. Any branch in Me that does not bear fruit [that stops bearing] He cuts away (trims off, takes away); and He cleanses and repeatedly prunes every branch that continues to bear fruit, to make it bear more and richer and more excellent fruit.*

You are cleansed and pruned already, because of the word which I have given you [the teachings I have discussed with you]. Dwell in Me, and I will dwell in you. [Live in Me, and I will live in you.] Just as no branch can bear fruit of itself without abiding in (being vitally united to) the vine, neither can you bear fruit unless you abide in Me.

I am the Vine; you are the branches. Whoever lives in Me and I in him bears much (abundant) fruit. However, apart from Me [cut off from vital union with Me] you can do nothing.

Prayers:

- Thank You, Father, that I have been born again and made a new creation in Christ

- Thank You, that I am part of Your family, accepted in Christ, indwelt by the Holy Spirit and saved, so that your good works can be commenced in my life

- I thank you because you are not a stagnant God. You desire that we grow in grace and in spiritual strength, in recognition and knowledge and in understanding of our Lord and Saviour Jesus Christ

- Father we know from your word that You are glorified when we bear much fruit and that we truly become Your disciples when we follow your will and ways. Father enable me to bear fruits of righteousness and of soul winning in Jesus name

- Enable me to be planted in the house of the Lord that I may flourish in the courts of God. Enable me to ever green (fresh growth) and be full of energy

- Father enable me to be like a tree planted by streams of water that yields its fruit in its season whose leaf does not wither and whatsoever I do, prospers. Enable me to be rooted in the word and to be intimate with the Spirit of God that I may prosper in all things

- Heavenly Father, I Thank You, that You have given me everything that is needed for godly living and a fruitful life. I pray that You would remove any area in my life that may hinder me from being fruitful in Your service

- Enable me to escape the corruption of this world system and empowers me to overcome the desires of the flesh

- Father keep me I pray, from being swayed by the deceit of the enemy who masquerades as an angel-of-light, and yet is a roaring lion, seeking whom he may devour

- Lord Jesus, I pray that I may grow in grace and increase in Christlikeness day by day. I pray for more fruitfulness and ability to grow more like the Lord Jesus Christ, with each passing day

- Lord, I know that there is much within me that needs to be rooted out, refined and removed and I ask that You examine my inner heart to discover any area of my life that needs to be corrected

- Help me Oh Lord, to depend on you without reservation, so that my life may become increasingly fruitful in each area that is lacking

- Lord, I know that in myself, I'm not capable and that only as I abide in Christ and depend on Him can the Holy Spirit make my life fruitful. I pray that I abide in You daily and bear much fruit to glorify your name.

- I am filled with the fruit of righteousness; as I live in loving dependence on You alone, and I pray that the fruit of the Spirit be manifested in all I say and do, to Your praise and glory in Jesus' name

- Heavenly Father, it is my desire to live a fruitful life in Christ. Keep me from walking in the counsel of ungodly men and women. I am preserved from the path of sinners and not be influenced by those that scorn the truth of God's Word. Rather, I delight in Your Word and meditate on its truth day and night

- From henceforth, I develop a fruit-filled life, looking to Jesus day by day. I depend on His sufficient grace, trust His Word moment by moment and maintain my hope in Him alone as the author and finisher of my faith in Jesus name

Scriptures for further prayers
John 15:8, Psalm 92:13-14, Philippians 1:11

DAY 20

PROSPERITY BY THE LORD

Worship

Today's Scripture and Meditation

Psalms 1:1. (NKJV): *Blessed is the man who walks not in the counsel of the ungodly, nor stands in the path of sinners, nor sits in the seat of the scornful; But his delight is in the law of the Lord, and in His law he meditates day and night. He shall be like a tree Planted by the rivers of water, that brings forth its fruit in its season, whose leaf also shall not wither; and whatever he does shall prosper*

Prayers:

- Father Lord, I thank you for giving me life today

- Father, empower me to speak, study, mediate (day and night) and be obedient to your Word so that I will prosper and have good success

- Lord Jesus, thank you for the finished work of Calvary which made it possible for your righteousness to be imputed unto me and to be counted among the righteous

- I receive grace not to walk in the counsel of the ungodly, nor stand in the path of sinners, nor sit in the seat of the scornful

- I receive grace to live and conduct myself in a manner that is worthy of you; such that every area of my life will be pleasing unto you

- Let the whole of my desire be to please you in all things: let the words of my mouth, the meditations of my heart and the actions that I take, be acceptable in Your sight, O Lord

- Enable me to grow unto maturity in godliness of mind and character, let me reach the height of virtue and integrity, even as you are perfect

- Father enable me to be alert and on my guard. I choose to stand firm in my faith and in my convictions - respecting Your precepts and keeping your sound doctrine

- Enable me to delight in your word all the days of my life

- God Almighty, let good success manifest in every area of my life so that your name can be glorified in me

- Your word says that righteous shall flourish like the evergreen palm tree. Father, enable me to be independent of circumstances but give me divine grace to live and thrive where all things else perish

- Enable me to grow big, strong, durable, beautiful, incorruptible and useful like the cedar of Lebanon

- Enable me to be planted, firmly rooted and prospering in the house of the Lord

- Enable me to prosper in all I do in the family, work, calling, ministry, and in every facet of my life in Jesus name

- Let me not be lacking in physical and spiritual supply because you are my source and sustainer. I shall not wither away in any aspects of my life – I am enabled and empowered to bring forth much for every of my labour in and out of season. I declare that I prosper in all things in Jesus name

Scriptures for further prayers

Psalms 92:12-14, Joshua 1:8

DAY 21

THANKSGIVING FOR EVERYTHING

Worship:

Today's Scripture

Psalms 75:1: *We give thanks to You, O God, we give thanks! For Your wondrous works declare that Your name is near.*

1Thessalonians5:18 (AMPC): *Thank [God] in everything [no matter what the circumstances may be, be thankful and give thanks], for this is the will of God for you [who are] in Christ Jesus [the Revealer and Mediator of that will]*

Prayer:

- Heavenly Father, You are worthy of thanksgiving

- Thank you in everything no matter what the circumstances are or have been

- Thank you for when I had little, thank you when there was nothing and I'm grateful for when I had plenty

- Thank You for the hope You bring through the toughest of times and the good times. Thank you Lord for you make all things works together for my good

- I thank you for Jesus for always being there at my sides. You know my heart, struggles and pains, Lord. Thank you for your sustaining presence and peace

- Thank You for your amazing power and work in my life and for Your goodness and blessings over me

- Thank You for Your great love that never fails in my life and for your care, for all that You do, for all You've given. Thank You for always being with me and never leaving me

- Thank you for your incredible sacrifice You made that I might have freedom and life. I appreciate you, Lord, for Your mercy and grace

- Thank you everlasting Father for Your countless blessings and for the challenges that draw us near to you. Thank You for the hard moments when You gave me the strength to wait in the midst of the storm

- Thank you for your sustenance and your light that surrounds me in times of storm. I acknowledge that You are my Rock and my Shelter

- Thank you for your joy and peace in the days of success, progress and prosperity

- Thank you for drawing me close this season and for renewing my spirit, reviving my soul and filling me daily with Your peace and joy

- I thank you Lord that my life shall make evident the fragrance of the knowledge of God everywhere

- I will proclaim your wonders tirelessly, for you alone deserve the glory and honour

- I love You and I need You, this day and every day

- I give You praise and adore you for your faithfulness and love, Lord. You alone are worthy to be praised in Jesus' Name, Amen

Scriptures for further prayers

2 Corinthians 2:14, Job 5:12, Psalm 28:7

WORDS FOR WORSHIP

God who is Love:

God You are love, You are life

Your love for us, is unfathomable

It's an immeasurable and everlasting love

I am grateful Lord, if not for Your love, where will we be?

I would have been meat for the enemy

I would have been gone and forgotten

You are the loving Father.

You love me so much

You sent your only begotten son to die for me

Your unconditional love grants unto me acceptance

Your love that breaks barriers and does not deplete

I worship You Lord and adore You

Lord Jesus, I honour you.

No greater love than this for a man to die for his friend.

It was love that took you to calvary

My Saviour and My Closest Friend

You ransomed souls and bought the nations

You saved my soul from the pending destruction

You reconciled me back to the father

There is no way to measure your worth

My redeemer I worship you

Great and Powerful God:

I worship you lord

You are Great and Powerful God,

Great in battle, Grace in glory

Great in Zion and greatly to the praised.

You are above all kings

You are above all powers

You are above all rulers

You are above all government

You are above all nature

You are above all created things

You are above all knowledge

You are above all wisdom

You are above all the ways of man

You are above all the creation of man

You are above all the invention of man

You are above all the knowledge of man

You are above all kingdoms

You are above all thrones, we worship You

You are above all wonders that we have ever known

You are above every possession

You are above every achievement

I lift You high far above, far above all, we lift You high

I stand in awe of Your majesty; I stand in awe of Your power.

Great, in favour, great in wonder

We worship You Lord

You are seated in majesty

Far above principalities and powers

Before You, all principalities, and powers they bow.

We worship this Limitless God, uncontainable God.

The great God who is interested in mere mortal men

We worship you in the firmament of Your power

Blessed be your name oh God

The Victorious God:

I worship you Lord because you are the Lord of Host,

The captain of the army of heaven

The victorious Lord.

You have won the victory

Death could not hold You down

You rose again that I might have victory over death

You are the victorious Lord, mighty in battle, fearful in praises

You are the one that goes to battle to win.

You have never lost a battle.

You are the victorious God

You conquered death

You conquered sickness

You conquered Satan and you have the key of hell and hades

You are given the name that is above every name

At your name every knee bows

Every tongue confess that Jesus Christ is Lord

To the glory of God the Father

I acknowledge you as Lord enthroned forever in Jesus name.

Amen!

God Our Father:

You are the Father of compassion

You are the father of our spirit

You are the Father of the heavenly lives

You are the Father of the fatherless

I bless Your holy name.

Our Father, You are the Faithful Father

The Gracious Father

The Awesome Father

The Father, with an open heart

The Forgiving Father

The committed Father

The caring Father

The responsible Father

My heavenly Father

Blessed be Your name forever.

ABOUT THE AUTHOR

Toyin Taiwo is the Senior Pastor of Grace Chapel Chesterfield, a growing multicultural church in the town of Chesterfield UK.

She graduated from Bible College in 1996 and she has been in ministry since then. She is a sound teacher of the Word. Through her cutting edge revelations and divine instructions in admonishing others to apply simple biblical principles, the lives of many have been impacted.

Her ministry is characterized by her compassionate and loving heart, which makes her to frequently intercede for people, cities, and nations.

Her pastoral heart has empowered her commitment to this sacrificial call upon her life. She is passionate about bringing the Grace of God unto everyone, reaching and making disciples of all mankind with the Good News of Jesus Christ, regardless of race, social or economic status.

Toyin is committed to changing the world one person at a time and to seeing "the church" (Christ's Body) grow and produce true Christians that will light up the world by exceptional Christian living.

Toyin is well known as an international public speaker in conferences, seminars, and leadership trainings all over Europe and North America. Through her prophetic declarations across the nations, lives have been changed and transformed by the power of God.

She is married to Debo Taiwo and they are blessed with children.

OTHER BOOKS

This book was written out of an experience of 365 days of speaking in tongues and listening to God, submitting to His will and obeying Him.

It is an anointed prayer devotional with the capacity to renew and revive any Christian who desires a consistent walk with God or desires next level of intimacy with Christ in 365 days.

The book is borne out of several meetings and LIVE experiences through which many have received the baptism and gifts of the Holy Spirit.

After this experience, lives have been changed ministries and callings have been birthed, threshing floor has been cleared, making room for God's manifestation in their lives. Also, other facets of life were attended to bring all round healing and health.

"I woke up one beautiful Friday summer morning of July 2019 and noticed a sharp pain in my chest; just under the bust on both sides and I was severely breathless. Based on the amount of pain I was in; I knew I needed to see a GP urgently.

This book is a record of what I experienced physically, emotionally and spiritually and what I learnt during the six months of medical investigations, while I prayed and hoped for healing."

Alive By Grace was written to build up our faith in the healing power of God, so that we can lay claim to our divine healing which was concluded over 2000 years ago on the cross of Calvary

You can order these books from toyintaiwo.org or from Amazon.

NOTES